GRAMMAR, SPELLING AND PUNCTUATION

SATs TESTS

YEAR 4

SCHOLASTIC

Book End, Range Road, Witney, Oxfordshire, OX29 0YD

www.scholastic.co.uk

© 2018 Scholastic Ltd

1 2 3 4 5 6 7 8 9   8 9 0 1 2 3 4 5 6 7

A British Library Cataloguing-in-Publication Data
A catalogue record for this book is available from the
British Library.

ISBN 978-1407-18295-7

Printed and bound by Ashford Colour Press

Author

Catherine Casey

Series consultants

Lesley and Graham Fletcher

Editorial team

Rachel Morgan, Tracey Cowell, Anna Hall,
Maggie Donovan, Shelley Welsh, Helen Lewis and Liz Evans

Design team

Nicolle Thomas, Neil Salt and Oxford Designers and Illustrators

Cover illustrations

Istock/calvindexter and Tomek.gr / Shutterstock/Visual Generation

Acknowledgements

Extracts from Department for Education website ©
Crown Copyright. Reproduced under the terms of the
Open Government Licence (OGL). www.nationalarchives.
gov.uk/doc/open-government-licence/version/3/

Every effort has been made to trace copyright holders
for the works reproduced in this publication, and the
publishers apologise or any inadvertent omissions.

Contents
Grammar, Punctuation & Spelling: Year 4

Contents	Page
Introduction	
About this book	4
Advice for parents and carers	5
Advice for children	6
Test coverage table	7
Tests	
Test A	10
Test B	32
Test C	54
Marks & guidance	
Marking and assessing the papers	76
Mark schemes for Test A	**78**
• Paper 1: Questions	78
• Paper 2: Spelling test script	81
Mark schemes for Test B	**84**
• Paper 1: Questions	84
• Paper 2: Spelling test script	87
Mark schemes for Test C	**90**
• Paper 1: Questions	90
• Paper 2: Spelling test script	93

About this book

This book provides you with practice papers to help support children with end-of-year tests.

Using the practice papers

The practice papers in this book can be used as you would any other practice materials. The children will need to be familiar with specific test-focused skills, such as reading carefully, leaving questions until the end if they seem too difficult, working at a suitable pace and checking through their work.

About the tests

Each Grammar, Punctuation & Spelling test for Year 4 has two parts:

- a short-answer Grammar, Punctuation and Vocabulary test, lasting 45 minutes
- a spelling test lasting around 15 minutes (although this is untimed).

This book provides three different tests and mark schemes.

The script for the spelling task for each paper can be found towards the end of the book.

Advice for parents and carers

How this book will help

This book will support your child to get ready for school-based end-of-year tests in Grammar, Punctuation & Spelling. It provides valuable practice of content expected of Year 4 children aged 8–9 years.

In the weeks leading up to the school tests, your child may be given practice, revision and tips to give them the best possible chance to demonstrate their knowledge and understanding. It is important to try to practise outside of school and many children benefit from extra input. This book will help your child prepare, and build their confidence and ability to work to a time limit. Practice is vital and every opportunity helps, so don't start too late.

In this book you will find three Grammar, Punctuation & Spelling tests. The layout and format of each test closely matches those used in the National Tests, so your child will become familiar with what to expect and get used to the style of the tests. There is a comprehensive answer section and guidance about how to mark the questions.

Tips

- Make sure that you allow your child to take the tests in a quiet environment where they are not likely to be interrupted or distracted.
- Make sure your child has a flat surface to work on with plenty of space to spread out and good light.
- Emphasise the importance of reading and re-reading a question, and to underline or circle any important information.
- These papers are similar to the ones your child will take in May in Year 6 and they therefore give you a good idea of strengths and areas for development. So, when you have found areas that require some more practice, it is useful to go over these again and practise similar types of question with your child.
- Go through the tests again together, identify any gaps in learning and address any misconceptions or areas of misunderstanding. If you are unsure of anything yourself, then make an appointment to see your child's teacher who will be able to help and advise further.

Advice for children

What to do before the tests

- Revise and practise on a regular basis.
- Spend some time each week practising.
- Focus on the areas you are least confident in to get better.
- Get a good night's sleep and eat a wholesome breakfast.
- Be on time for school.
- Have all the necessary materials.
- Avoid stressful situations before a test.

Test coverage table

Paper 1: Grammar, Punctuation & Vocabulary: Year 4

The children will need to be familiar with and be able to demonstrate use of the following, including correct use and understanding of the terminology.

	Content
Grammatical words and word classes	Nouns
	Verbs
	Adjectives
	Conjunctions
	Pronouns Possessive pronouns
	Adverbs Adverbials Fronted adverbials
	Prepositions
	Determiners
Functions of sentences	Statements Questions Exclamations Commands
Combining words, phrases and clauses	Sentences Clauses
	Noun phrases
	Co-ordinating conjunctions Subordinating conjunctions Subordinate clauses
	Simple past and simple present tense Verbs in the perfect form Present and past progressive tense Tense consistency

	Content
Punctuation	Capital letters Full stops Question marks Exclamation marks
	Commas in lists Commas after fronted adverbials
	Inverted commas
	Apostrophes for contraction Apostrophes for possession
Vocabulary	Prefixes Suffixes Word families
Standard English and formality	Standard English

Grammar, Punctuation & Spelling

Tests A, B and C

Grammar, Punctuation & Spelling

Test A, Paper 1: Questions

Questions and answers

You have 45 minutes to complete this paper. There are different types of question for you to answer in different ways. The space for your answer shows you what type of answer is needed. Write your answer in the space provided.

- **Multiple choice answers:** for some questions you do not need to do any writing. Read the instructions carefully so you know how to answer the question.
- **Short answers:** some questions are followed by a line or a box. This shows you need to write a word, a few words or a sentence.

Marks

The number of marks in the margin tells you the maximum number of marks for each question.

You should work through the paper until you are asked to stop.

Work as quickly and as carefully as you can. If you finish before the end, go back and check your work.

You will have 45 minutes to answer the questions in this paper.

1. Circle the words that should begin with a **capital letter** in the sentence below.

on friday eva went running.

Marks

1

2. Underline the two **nouns** in this sentence.

The teacher gave out sparkly stickers.

1

3. Tick the sentence which includes two **adjectives**.

Tick **one**.

The girls were playing in the long grass. ☐

The girls were playing in the long, green grass. ☐

The girls were always playing in the long grass. ☐

1

4. Circle the **adverb** in this sentence.

The boy stood on the stage confidently.

1

	Marks

5. Which sentence uses **commas in a list** correctly?

Tick **one**.

I played on the swing, and the slide, and the climbing frame. ☐

I played on the swing, the slide and the climbing frame. ☐

I played on, the swing, the slide and the climbing frame. ☐

1

6. Tick one box in each row to show whether the sentence is in the **past tense** or the **present tense**.

	Past tense	Present tense
The enormous dog barked at the postwoman.		
I walk to school.		
The baby slept in his cot.		

1

7. Complete the sentence below using an appropriate **adjective**.

The girl wore a _____ dress.

1

8. Circle the correct **verb form** to complete this sentence.

Rosie **am** / **are** / **were** / **was** running late for football practice but we started anyway.

Marks

1

9. Underline the **co-ordinating conjunction** in this sentence.

It was a hot day and the children were playing in the garden.

1

10. Draw lines to match each sentence to the correct **sentence type**.

What a mess your room is!	Statement
Could you tidy your room?	Command
Tidy up this mess now.	Question
There are a lot of things on your bedroom floor.	Exclamation

1

Marks

11. Add the **prefix** *dis* to these words. Write the new word in the box. One has been done for you.

	New word
obey	disobey
appear	
agree	
like	

1

---

12. What type of **adverb** is <u>soon</u>?

Tick **one**.

Adverb of time ☐

Adverb of place ☐

Adverb of cause ☐

1

---

13. Insert a **comma** in the correct place in the sentence below.

I go to dance lessons on Saturdays Sundays and Tuesdays.

1

14. Add the **suffix** *er* to change these verbs to nouns. Write the new word in the box. One has been done for you.

You may need to add or subtract letters.

Verb	Noun
teach	teacher
dance	
run	

Marks

1

15. Draw lines to match the words below to the correct **contraction**. One has been done for you.

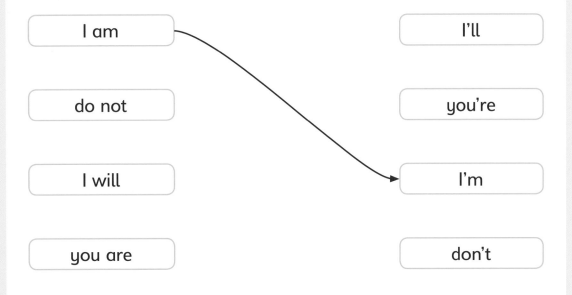

I am	I'll
do not	you're
I will	I'm
you are	don't

1

Marks

16. Underline the **noun phrase** in this sentence.

He ate the last chocolate cupcake.

1

17. Circle the **subordinating conjunction** in this sentence.

The children splashed in the puddles when it rained.

1

18. Tick one box in each row to show whether the **apostrophe** is for **possession** or **contraction**.

	Possession	Contraction
I don't like swimming.		
The teacher found Adam's PE bag.		
You're really good at swimming.		

1

19. Which sentence uses the **present progressive form** of the verb?

Marks

Tick **one**.

I was running in the playground. ☐

I am running in the playground. ☐

I ran in the playground. ☐

1

20. Where should the missing **inverted commas** go in the sentence below? Tick **two** boxes.

☐   ☐ ☐   ☐

Line up please, said the teacher.

1

21. Circle the **preposition** in this sentence.

I saw a shiny, blue bike in the shop window.

Marks

1

22. Tick one box in each row to show whether the **main clause** or the **subordinate clause** is in bold.

	Main clause	Subordinate clause
I saw a beautiful rainbow in the sky **when the sun shone**.		
When it rained, **the children splashed in the puddles**.		
We had a picnic outside **because it was sunny**.		

1

Marks

23. Sort these words into **word families**. Write them in the table below.

| solution | dissolve | children |
| insoluble | childlike | childish |

child	solve

1

24. Which sentence uses **inverted commas** correctly?

Tick **one**.

"What is the time please?" asked Farah. ☐

"What is the time please"? asked Farah. ☐

"What is the time please? asked Farah." ☐

1

Marks

25. Circle the correct **determiner** to complete the sentence below.

The girl chose **a** / **an** pear from the fruit bowl.

1

26. Which sentence uses **Standard English**?

Tick **one**.

The birds sing beautifully. ☐

The bird sing beautifully. ☐

The birds sings beautifully. ☐

1

27. Insert a **comma** in the correct place in the sentence below.

While at the park I played on the swings.

1

Marks

28. Circle the **determiner** in this sentence.

I am going to tidy my room.

1

29. Start this sentence with a **fronted adverbial**.

_____, the children sheltered

from the rain.

1

30. Rewrite this sentence in the **present tense**.

The dog barked at the cat.

_____

1

31. Which of these sentences is a **command**?

Tick **one**.

You need to tidy your room. ☐

Let's tidy your room together. ☐

Tidy your room. ☐

1

Marks

32. Choose the correct verb to complete this sentence in the **past tense**.

| hop   hopped   hops   hopping |

The frog _____ into the pond.

1

33. Rewrite this statement as a **question**.

Lessons start at 9 o'clock.

_____

1

34. Circle the **adverbial** in the sentence below.

The little boy ran to the finish line as fast as he could.

1

35. Tick the sentence that uses **capital letters** correctly.

Marks

Tick **one**.

Yesterday, I had toast for breakfast. ☐

yesterday, i had toast for breakfast. ☐

yesterday, I had toast for breakfast. ☐

1

36. Choose the correct word to complete this sentence.

| girls   girl   girls'   girl's |

The _____ football kits had arrived and they felt excited about playing in the match on Saturday.

1

37. Insert the missing **punctuation mark** into the sentence.

"How old are you ☐" asked the lady behind the desk.

1

Test A, Paper 1: Questions

38. What type of word is <u>regularly</u> in the sentence below?

Flora visits her Gran <u>regularly</u>.

Tick one.

A verb ☐

An adverb ☐

An adjective ☐

Marks

1

39. Circle the **proper noun** in the sentence below.

The nurse measured Ava's temperature.

1

40. Underline the **verb** in the sentence below.

I went to the cinema at the weekend.

1

41. Draw a line to match the underlined text to the type of **phrase** it is.

I had <u>hot chocolate with marshmallows</u>

a noun phrase

hot chocolate with marshmallows

an adverbial phrase

a prepositional phrase

1

42. Circle the **conjunction** in the sentence below.

Before dinner, she washed her hands.

Marks

1

43. Use a **co-ordinating conjunction** to complete the sentence below.

You can borrow my sunglasses _____ be careful not to break them.

1

44. Underline the **pronoun** in the sentence below.

Callum was upset that he couldn't go to the party.

1

45. Tick the sentence that is an **exclamation**.

Marks

Tick **one**.

What a brilliant cartwheel the gymnast did ☐

The gymnast did a cartwheel ☐

Can you do a cartwheel ☐

1

46. Which sentence uses the **present perfect tense**?

Tick **one**.

Andrew went to rugby practice. ☐

Andrew has been to rugby practice before. ☐

Andrew is at rugby practice. ☐

1

47. Choose the **pair of verbs** that correctly completes the sentence below. Tick **one**.

The door _____ white but it _____ blue before the decorator painted it.

Tick **one**.

is   was ☐

was   is ☐

is   is ☐

1

Marks

48. Circle the **possessive pronoun** in the sentence below.

The last chocolate was mine.

1

49. Underline the **adverb** in this sentence.

Ella accidentally broke her mother's favourite vase.

1

50. Insert **inverted commas** to complete the sentence below.

What would you like to drink? asked the waiter.

1

End of paper

Grammar, Punctuation & Spelling

Test A, Paper 2: Spelling

Instructions

- Your **spelling** will be tested in this paper.

- **20 short sentences** will be read aloud to you. A single word has been missed out of each sentence and you need to write this in the space provided.

- **You will hear each word three times.** The word will be said once, then read within a sentence, then repeated a third time. You should write the spelling in the space provided.

- All 20 sentences will be read again at the end, when you will be able to make any changes you wish to what you have written down.

- This paper should take approximately **15 minutes** to complete, although you will be allowed as much time as you need to complete the test.

■SCHOLASTIC National Curriculum SATs Tests

1. In _____, it snowed heavily for days.

2. Can you _____ the cheese?

3. The builder needed to _____ the room.

4. I had to make a _____ about which after-school club to go to.

5. The tour guide gave us lots of _____ about the museum.

6. The girl danced _____ across the room.

7. The sign was _____ because it pointed in the wrong direction.

8. The teacher said the answer was _____.

9. My sister ate the last _____ of fruit.

10. Although they are twins, Mia and Ava are quite _____.

Test A, Paper 2: Spelling

11. I _____ to do my homework.

12. I had _____ for dinner.

13. The boy read his magazine with _____.

14. _____ flying to the moon in a rocket.

15. We learned how to _____ a wall.

16. I borrowed a book from the _____.

17. My _____ colour is blue.

18. _____ is good for your body and heart.

19. There was a car _____ on the motorway.

20. I can't _____ my password to log on to the computer.

End of paper

Question		Focus	Possible marks	Actual marks
Paper 1	1	Punctuation: capital letters	1	
	2	Grammar: nouns	1	
	3	Grammar: adjectives	1	
	4	Grammar: adverbs	1	
	5	Punctuation: commas in a list	1	
	6	Grammar: past and present tense	1	
	7	Grammar: adjectives	1	
	8	Grammar: verbs	1	
	9	Grammar: co-ordinating conjunctions	1	
	10	Grammar: sentence types	1	
	11	Vocabulary: prefixes	1	
	12	Grammar: adverbs	1	
	13	Punctuation: commas in a list	1	
	14	Vocabulary: suffixes	1	
	15	Punctuation: apostrophes for contraction	1	
	16	Grammar: noun phrases	1	
	17	Grammar: subordinating conjunctions	1	
	18	Punctuation: apostrophes for possession and contraction	1	
	19	Grammar: progressive verb form	1	
	20	Punctuation: inverted commas	1	
	21	Grammar: prepositions	1	
	22	Grammar: main and subordinate clauses	1	
	23	Vocabulary: word families	1	
	24	Punctuation: inverted commas	1	
	25	Grammar: determiners	1	
	26	Grammar: Standard English	1	
	27	Punctuation: commas after fronted adverbials	1	
	28	Grammar: determiners	1	
	29	Grammar: fronted adverbials	1	
	30	Grammar: present tense	1	
	31	Grammar: commands	1	
	32	Grammar: past tense	1	
	33	Grammar: questions	1	
	34	Grammar: adverbials	1	
	35	Punctuation: capital letters	1	
	36	Punctuation: apostrophes for possession	1	
	37	Punctuation: question marks	1	
	38	Grammar: adverbs	1	
	39	Grammar: nouns	1	
	40	Grammar: verbs	1	
	41	Grammar: noun phrases	1	
	42	Grammar: conjunctions	1	
	43	Grammar: co-ordinating conjunctions	1	
	44	Grammar: pronouns	1	
	45	Punctuation: exclamations	1	
	46	Grammar: present perfect	1	
	47	Grammar: tense consistency	1	
	48	Grammar: possessive pronouns	1	
	49	Grammar: adverbs	1	
	50	Punctuation: inverted commas	1	
Paper 2	1–20	Spelling	20	
		Total	**70**	

Test B, Paper 1: Questions

Questions and answers

You have 45 minutes to complete this paper. There are different types of question for you to answer in different ways. The space for your answer shows you what type of answer is needed. Write your answer in the space provided.

- **Multiple choice answers:** for some questions you do not need to do any writing. Read the instructions carefully so you know how to answer the question.

- **Short answers:** some questions are followed by a line or a box. This shows you need to write a word, a few words or a sentence.

Marks

The number of marks in the margin tells you the maximum number of marks for each question.

You should work through the paper until you are asked to stop.

Work as quickly and as carefully as you can. If you finish before the end, go back and check your work.

You will have 45 minutes to answer the questions in this paper.

1. Circle the two **nouns** in this sentence.

The little brown hamster had escaped from his cage.

Marks

1

2. Read the sentence below. What **type of word** is the word <u>pink</u>?

We had a picnic with cheese sandwiches, delicious <u>pink</u> cakes, crisps and grapes.

Tick **one**.

A verb ☐

A noun ☐

An adverb ☐

An adjective ☐

1

Marks

3. Draw lines to match each sentence to the correct **sentence type**.

| Would you like a drink? | Statement |

| I had a drink. | Command |

| What a refreshing drink that was! | Question |

| Get me a drink. | Exclamation |

1

4. Circle the words that should begin with a **capital letter** in the sentence below.

on wednesdays i have drumming lessons.

1

5. Underline the three **adjectives** in this sentence.

The new computer was large and gleaming.

1

6. Tick one box in each row to show the correct **punctuation mark** to complete each sentence.

Marks

	Full stop	Question mark
When will the football match start		
When we walked to school, it was very cold		
When can I eat my lunch		

1

7. Circle the best **conjunction** to complete this sentence.

I didn't like my lunch **and** / **but** / **or** I enjoyed

the pudding.

1

8. Read the sentence below. What **type of word** is the word <u>nest</u>?

The bird flew to its <u>nest</u> at the top of the tree.

Tick **one**.

A verb ☐

An adjective ☐

A noun ☐

An adverb ☐

1

9. Choose the correct **verb form** to complete this sentence. Write it in the space.

| played | plays | playing | play |

We were _____ in the garden.

1

Marks

10. Insert a **comma** in the correct place in the sentence below.

I packed an umbrella Wellington boots and a coat.

1

11. Circle the correct **verb form** to complete this sentence.

The boy **am** / **are** / **were** / **was** singing.

1

12. Draw lines to join each **prefix** to a word to change its meaning.

un		possible
im		happy
dis		correct
in		like

1

13. Which sentence uses **commas in a list** correctly?

Tick **one**.

I had sandwiches, an apple and a drink for lunch. ☐

I had sandwiches and an apple and a drink for lunch. ☐

I had sandwiches, and an apple, and a drink for lunch. ☐

Marks

1

14. Underline the **noun phrase** in this sentence.

My sister took the last piece of fruit.

1

15. Add the **suffix** ly to change these adjectives to adverbs. Write the new word in the box. One has been done for you.

Adjective	Adverb
slow	slowly
quick	
careful	
excited	

1

16. Which sentence uses an **apostrophe for possession** correctly?

Marks

Tick **one**.

The teacher found Annie,s lunchbox in the hall. ☐

The teacher found Annie's lunchbox in the hall. ☐

The teacher found Annies' lunchbox in the hall. ☐

1

17. Fill the gaps in the sentence below, using the **past progressive** form of the verbs shown in the boxes.

| to read |

While I _____ a book, my sister

_____ with her toy car.

| to play |

1

Grammar, Punctuation & Spelling

Test B, Paper 1: Questions

18. Complete this sentence with a suitable **adverb**.

The cat miaowed _____.

Marks

1

19. Draw lines to match the words below to the correct **contraction**. One has been done for you.

has not	we'll
does not	they're
we will	hasn't
they are	doesn't

1

Marks

20. Which is the most appropriate **conjunction** to introduce the **subordinate clause** in this sentence?

I wanted to go to school _____ I wasn't feeling very well.

Tick **one**.

furthermore ☐

even though ☐

because ☐

1

21. Circle the **preposition** in this sentence.

I woke up before my alarm clock.

1

22. Look at the **root words**. Write two words from each **word family** in the table below.

Root word	Word family
appear	
cycle	

1

Test B, Paper 1: Questions

23. In the sentence below, underline the **main clause** and circle the **subordinate clause**.

It hurt when I fell over in the playground.

Marks

1

24. Choose the correct **determiner** to complete the sentence below.

| a | an |

At playtime I had _____ orange.

1

25. Where should the missing **inverted commas** go in the sentence below? Tick **two** boxes.

Are we nearly there yet? asked the little boy.

1

Marks

26. Circle the correct **pronoun** to complete this sentence.

Khaled went home early. He took **her** / **his** / **him** bag with him.

1

27. Insert a **comma** in the correct place in the sentence below.

As it was raining we played games in the classroom.

1

28. Underline the three **determiners** in this sentence.

That bird ate some seeds on the bird table.

1

29. Rewrite this sentence in the **past tense**.

I cook dinner for my friends.

_____

Marks

1

30. Put a tick in each row to show whether the sentence is a **statement**, a **question** or a **command**.

Sentence	Statement	Question	Command
When can we sit down			
Sit down			
It's great to sit down			

1

31. Choose the correct verb to complete this sentence in the **present tense**. Write it in the space.

sleeps   sleep   slept   sleeping

The baby _____ in her cot.

1

32. Rewrite this question as a **statement**.

Did you eat your sandwiches before you ate the cake?

_____

1

	Marks

33. The words in bold are a type of **adverbial**. What kind of adverbial are they?

At half time, the netball team had oranges.

_____

1

34. Circle the **verb** in the sentence below.

I have white shoes.

1

35. Underline the words that should have a **capital letter**.

"Can i play?" asked gemma.

1

36. Rewrite this passage, putting in all the **capital letters** and **full stops**.

"what time do you normally go to bed?" asked ajay

"usually around 8.00pm," replied isaac

_____

_____

1

37. Circle the **adverb** in the sentence below.

The children were playing outdoors.

Marks

1

38. Tick the sentence that should have an **exclamation mark**.

Tick **one**.

What an amazing day we've had ☐

What are you doing today ☐

1

39. Which sentence uses the **progressive past tense**?

Tick **one**.

George cried at lunchtime. ☐

George was crying at lunchtime. ☐

George is crying. ☐

1

40. Circle the correct word to complete the sentence using **Standard English**.

He ran through the woods **quick** / **quickly**.

1

41. Underline the **noun phrase** in this sentence.

I ate a boiled egg with a runny yolk for my breakfast.

1

42. Use a **co-ordinating conjunction** to complete this sentence.

and   but   so

I tidied my room _____ I could have my pocket money.

1

43. Circle the **possessive pronoun**.

"That is mine," shouted the child.

1

44. Rewrite the sentence so it has a **fronted adverbial**.

We read a story together after dinner.

1

45. Which **pair of verbs** correctly completes the sentence below?

People used to think that the world _____ flat but it is now known that it _____ round.

Tick **one**.

is   was   ☐

was   was   ☐

was   is   ☐

1

46. Rewrite this sentence using the **present perfect** form of the verb <u>wanted</u>.

Since last year, Cora wanted to be on the cricket team.

_____

_____

1

47. Rewrite the sentence below so that it begins with the **adverbial**. Use only the same words.

We had a picnic after swimming.

_____

1

48. Which sentence uses **inverted commas** correctly?

Marks

Tick **one**.

"Make sure all the litter goes in the bin please," said the teacher. ☐

"Make sure all the litter goes in the bin please, said the teacher." ☐

"Make sure all the litter goes in the bin please", said the teacher. ☐

1

49. Show the correct place to insert a **comma** in the sentence below. Tick **one** box.

☐   ☐   ☐

After school on Tuesdays I have judo and then football.

1

50. Insert **inverted commas** to complete the sentence below.

It is extremely likely to rain this afternoon, said the

weather presenter.

1

End of paper

Test B, Paper 2: Spelling

Instructions

- Your **spelling** will be tested in this paper.

- **20 short sentences** will be read aloud to you. A single word has been missed out of each sentence and you need to write this in the space provided.

- **You will hear each word three times.** The word will be said once, then read within a sentence, then repeated a third time. You should write the spelling in the space provided.

- All 20 sentences will be read again at the end, when you will be able to make any changes you wish to what you have written down.

- This paper should take approximately **15 minutes** to complete, although you will be allowed as much time as you need to complete the test.

1. _____ it will be sunny at the weekend.

2. The lion's _____ was long and fluffy.

3. I stuck the _____ onto the fridge.

4. I was watching _____.

5. Walking on the grass with bare feet was a strange

   _____.

6. _____, I finished my homework.

7. The teacher warned us not to _____

   on the school trip.

8. The test was _____.

9. Did you _____ that noise?

10. The shelves were covered in lots of plants and shrubs of

    _____ shapes and sizes.

11. The post had _____ on time.

12. I didn't _____ the story.

13. I woke up very _____ this morning.

14. Is there _____ paper for everyone?

15. Scissors don't just _____.

16. We saw the _____ outside Buckingham palace.

17. My cousin was very _____ at the supermarket.

18. I was allowed to stay up late as it was a _____ occasion.

19. We investigated which _____ would be best for an umbrella.

20. I would like to _____ Spanish.

End of paper

Question		Focus	Possible marks	Actual marks
Paper 1	1	Grammar: nouns	1	
	2	Grammar: adjectives	1	
	3	Grammar: sentence types	1	
	4	Punctuation: capital letters	1	
	5	Grammar: adjectives	1	
	6	Punctuation: full stops, question marks	1	
	7	Grammar: co-ordinating conjunctions	1	
	8	Grammar: nouns	1	
	9	Grammar: progressive verb	1	
	10	Punctuation: commas in a list	1	
	11	Grammar: Standard English	1	
	12	Vocabulary: prefixes	1	
	13	Punctuation: commas in a list	1	
	14	Grammar: noun phrases	1	
	15	Vocabulary: suffixes	1	
	16	Punctuation: apostrophes for possession	1	
	17	Grammar: progressive verb	1	
	18	Grammar: adverbs	1	
	19	Punctuation: apostrophes for contraction	1	
	20	Grammar: subordinating conjunctions	1	
	21	Grammar: prepositions	1	
	22	Vocabulary: word families	1	
	23	Grammar: main and subordinate clauses	1	
	24	Grammar: determiners	1	
	25	Punctuation: inverted commas	1	
	26	Grammar: possessive pronouns	1	
	27	Punctuation: commas after fronted adverbials	1	
	28	Grammar: determiners	1	
	29	Grammar: past tense	1	
	30	Grammar: questions, statements and commands	1	
	31	Grammar: present tense	1	
	32	Grammar: statements	1	
	33	Grammar: fronted adverbials	1	
	34	Grammar: verbs	1	
	35	Punctuation: capital letters	1	
	36	Punctuation: capital letters and full stops	1	
	37	Grammar: adverbs	1	
	38	Punctuation: exclamation marks	1	
	39	Grammar: progressive verb form	1	
	40	Grammar: Standard English	1	
	41	Grammar: expanded noun phrases	1	
	42	Grammar: co-ordinating conjunctions	1	
	43	Grammar: possessive pronouns	1	
	44	Grammar: fronted adverbials	1	
	45	Punctuation: tense consistency	1	
	46	Grammar: present perfect	1	
	47	Grammar: fronted adverbials	1	
	48	Punctuation: inverted commas	1	
	49	Punctuation: commas after fronted adverbials	1	
	50	Punctuation: inverted commas	1	
Paper 2	1–20	Spelling	20	
		Total	**70**	

Grammar, Punctuation & Spelling

Test C, Paper 1: Questions

Questions and answers

You have 45 minutes to complete this paper. There are different types of question for you to answer in different ways. The space for your answer shows you what type of answer is needed. Write your answer in the space provided.

- **Multiple choice answers:** for some questions you do not need to do any writing. Read the instructions carefully so you know how to answer the question.
- **Short answers:** some questions are followed by a line or a box. This shows you need to write a word, a few words or a sentence.

Marks

The number of marks in the margin tells you the maximum number of marks for each question.

You should work through the paper until you are asked to stop.

Work as quickly and as carefully as you can. If you finish before the end, go back and check your work.

You will have 45 minutes to answer the questions in this paper.

	Marks

1. Circle the two **nouns** in this sentence.

Zara ate a juicy pear.

1

2. Choose the best **punctuation mark** to complete each sentence. Write the punctuation in the boxes below. Use each punctuation mark **once**.

! ? .

When is it lunch time ☐

What a brilliant lunch ☐

Lunch is at 1 o'clock today ☐

1

3. Read the sentence below. What **type of word** is the word <u>scarf</u>?

Mum bought a lovely soft, green <u>scarf</u> from the shop.

Tick one.

A noun ☐

An adverb ☐

An adjective ☐

A verb ☐

1

4. Circle the three **adjectives** in this sentence.

The wind blew my favourite kite into the old oak tree.

Marks

1

5. Which **verb form** correctly completes this sentence?

We **was** / **were** / **am** running around the playground at lunchtime.

1

6. Sort these words into **adjectives** and **adverbs**. Write them in the table below. One has been done for you.

next   wobbly   ancient   shiny   gently   ~~carefully~~

Adjective	Adverb
	carefully

1

7. Circle the words that should begin with a **capital letter** in the sentence below.

last thursday, i went to the park.

Marks

1

8. Which ending would make this word an **adverb**?

happy

Tick **one**.

happi<u>er</u> ☐

happi<u>ly</u> ☐

happi<u>ness</u> ☐

happi<u>est</u> ☐

1

9. Which sentence uses **commas in a list** correctly?

Marks

Tick **one**.

I packed a towel, my goggles and a swimming costume. ☐

I packed a towel, and my goggles, and my swimming costume. ☐

I packed, a towel, my goggles, my swimming costume. ☐

1

10. Use the same **prefix** to change these words to their opposite meaning.

kind   ⟶   _____

pleasant ⟶   _____

happy   ⟶   _____

1

11. Use an **adverb of time** to complete this sentence.

_____, I go to my friend's house for tea.

1

12. Add the **suffix** *ation* to change these words. One has been done for you. You may need to subtract some letters.

	New word
prepare	preparation
sense	
admire	

1

13. Draw lines to match the words below to the correct **contraction**. One has been done for you.

she is	he's
he has	we're
I have	she's
we are	I've

1

Marks

14. Fill the gaps in the sentence below, using the **past progressive form** of the verbs shown in the boxes.

to read

I _____ my book while the teacher

_____ .

to talk

1

15. Underline the **noun phrase** in this sentence.

The tired little girl fell asleep on the way home.

1

16. Tick one box in each row to show whether the **apostrophe** is for **possession** or **contraction**.

	Possession	Contraction
I don't like art classes.		
The teacher found Jake's homework in his bag.		
Amira's ballet shoes were lost.		
I'm going to play netball at lunchtime.		

1

Marks

17. Underline the **main clause** in this sentence.

I didn't go to school today because I was unwell.

1

18. Which sentence uses **inverted commas** correctly?

Tick **one**.

"I have forgotten my PE kit, said Ted." ☐

"I have forgotten my PE kit", said Ted. ☐

"I have forgotten my PE kit," said Ted. ☐

1

19. Circle the **preposition** in this sentence.

The towels were on the bathroom shelf.

1

20. Underline the correct **determiners** to complete the sentence below.

We had **a / an** unusual fruit at snack time and **a / an** delicious orange drink.

Marks

1

21. Circle the correct **pronoun** in the passage below.

The children were going on a school trip to the zoo. To prepare for their trip, **he / she / they / we** had written down questions to ask the zookeeper.

1

22. Insert a **comma** in the correct place in the sentence below.

In the sunshine we sat and waited for our lunch.

1

23. Which sentence uses **Standard English**?

Tick **one**.

The boys was dancing. ☐

The boys were dancing. ☐

The boy were dancing. ☐

1

Marks

24. Circle the two **determiners** in this sentence.

There was a book token for every child.

1

25. Fill in the gap in the sentence below, using the **past tense** of the verb in the box.

to kiss

The frog _____ the pretty princess.

1

26. Rewrite this statement as a **command**.

You should go home.

_____

_____

1

27. Complete the table with the **present tense** of each verb. One has been done for you.

Present tense	Past tense
We know	We knew
	We drew
	We ran

1

28. Draw lines to match each sentence to the correct **sentence type**.

| Is it time to go to school? | | Statement |

| It's time to go to school. | | Exclamation |

| Go to school. | | Question |

| What an amazing school that is! | | Command |

1

29. Rewrite the sentence below so that it begins with the **adverbial**. Use only the same words.

My granny took me to the zoo last Sunday.

_____

1

30. **a.** Add the **prefix** *re* to these words.

	New word
turn	return
decorate	
appear	

1

b. How does the **prefix** *re* change the meaning of these words?

_____

_____

1

31. Tick the sentence that uses **capital letters** correctly.

Marks

Tick **one**.

The Eiffel Tower is in France. ☐

The eiffel tower is in France. ☐

The Eiffel Tower is in france. ☐

1

32. Insert **full stops** and **capital letters** in the correct places in the passage below.

when the children arrived at the airport, they were excited then they found out that their flight was delayed for two hours when they finally arrived in spain, they were very tired

1

33. Insert the missing **punctuation mark** into the sentence below.

"What are we having for lunch ☐" Rachel asked.

1

Marks

34. What type of word is <u>caught</u> in this sentence?

I <u>caught</u> the bus into town.

Tick **one**.

A verb ☐

An adverb ☐

An adjective ☐

1

35. Circle the **nouns** in the sentence below.

The optician tested my eyes.

1

36. Underline the **adverb** in the sentence below.

Often, I go swimming on Saturdays.

1

37. Draw a line to match the text to the type of phrase it is.

I made <u>a lovely cup of tea</u> for Gran.

a prepositional phrase

a lovely cup of tea

an adverbial phrase

a noun phrase

1

38. Underline the **conjunction** in the sentence below.

Because it was so hot, we put sun cream on.

Marks

1

39. Use a **co-ordinating conjunction** to complete the sentence below.

> but   so   and

You can visit the dinosaur museum _____ you mustn't touch anything.

1

40. Circle the **pronouns** in the sentence below.

We had ice creams and they all had chocolate sauce on top.

1

41. Tick the sentence that is an **exclamation**.

Marks

Tick **one**.

What a wonderful party I went to ☐

I went to a party ☐

What time is the party ☐

1

42. Which sentence uses the **present perfect tense**?

Tick **one**.

Aryan went to the dentist. ☐

Aryan has been waiting the longest. ☐

Aryan is waiting at the dentist. ☐

1

43. Change these sentence to the **past tense**.

We write emails to our grandparents.

_____

We draw pictures when we get bored.

_____

1

44. Circle the **possessive pronoun** in the sentences below.

At the shop we all bought new hats. Mine is blue.

Marks

1

45. Which sentence uses **inverted commas** correctly?

Tick **one**.

"I was second in the skipping race on Sports Day, said Sally" happily. ☐

"I was second in the skipping race on Sports Day," said Sally happily. ☐

"I was second in the skipping race on Sports Day, said Sally happily." ☐

1

46. Insert a **comma** in the correct place in the sentence below.

After painting wash the brushes with warm water.

1

Test C, Paper 1: Questions

47. Insert **inverted commas** into the sentence below.

Marks

No running by the pool, said the lifeguard.

1

48. Rewrite the sentence below so that it begins with the **adverbial**. Use only the same words.

The rocket launched into space after the countdown.

_____

_____

1

49. Circle the correct word to complete this sentence using **Standard English**.

The children **was** / **were** having a picnic at the park.

1

End of paper

Test C, Paper 2: Spelling

Instructions

- Your **spelling** will be tested in this paper.

- **20 short sentences** will be read aloud to you. A single word has been missed out of each sentence and you need to write this in the space provided.

- **You will hear each word three times.** The word will be said once, then read within a sentence, then repeated a third time. You should write the spelling in the space provided.

- All 20 sentences will be read again at the end, when you will be able to make any changes you wish to what you have written down.

- This paper should take approximately **15 minutes** to complete, although you will be allowed as much time as you need to complete the test.

Grammar, Punctuation & Spelling

Test C, Paper 2: Spelling

1. My cousin damaged the kite on _____.

2. I hoped the wobbly chair would not _____.

3. There was a tiny red and black _____ crawling on the window sill.

4. The _____ began in the middle of the night.

5. The _____ of your work is important.

6. I _____ put the ladybird back outside.

7. I was lost because I had _____ the directions.

8. I _____ with my brother's choice of television programme.

9. The autumn _____ were blowing around the playground.

10. I will _____ my answer.

11. I held my _____.

12. I finally _____ my homework.

13. "Please _____," said the teacher.

14. I want to be a _____ singer.

15. I was facing _____ on the train.

16. I _____ a strange noise outside.

17. Exercise raises your _____ rate.

18. The boat arrived at the desert _____.

19. It was just an _____ day.

20. The _____ were chatting loudly in the cafe.

End of paper

Test C: Marks

Question		Focus	Possible marks	Actual marks
Paper 1	1	Grammar: nouns	1	
	2	Punctuation: full stops, question marks, exclamation marks	1	
	3	Grammar: nouns	1	
	4	Grammar: adjectives	1	
	5	Grammar: Standard English	1	
	6	Grammar: adjectives and adverbs	1	
	7	Punctuation: capital letters	1	
	8	Grammar: adverbs	1	
	9	Punctuation: commas in a list	1	
	10	Vocabulary: prefixes	1	
	11	Grammar: adverbs of time	1	
	12	Vocabulary: suffixes	1	
	13	Punctuation: apostrophes for contraction	1	
	14	Grammar: progressive verb form	1	
	15	Grammar: noun phrases	1	
	16	Punctuation: apostrophes	1	
	17	Grammar: main and subordinate clauses	1	
	18	Punctuation: inverted commas	1	
	19	Grammar: prepositions	1	
	20	Grammar: determiners	1	
	21	Grammar: pronouns	1	
	22	Punctuation: commas after fronted adverbials	1	
	23	Grammar: Standard English	1	
	24	Grammar: determiners	1	
	25	Grammar: past tense	1	
	26	Grammar: commands	1	
	27	Grammar: present tense	1	
	28	Grammar: statements, exclamations, questions, commands	1	
	29	Grammar: fronted adverbials	1	
	30	Vocabulary: prefixes	2	
	31	Punctuation: capital letters	1	
	32	Punctuation: full stops and capital letters	1	
	33	Punctuation: question marks	1	
	34	Grammar: verbs	1	
	35	Grammar: nouns	1	
	36	Grammar: adverbs	1	
	37	Grammar: noun phrases	1	
	38	Grammar: conjunctions	1	
	39	Grammar: co-ordinating conjunctions	1	
	40	Grammar: pronouns	1	
	41	Punctuation: exclamations	1	
	42	Grammar: present perfect	1	
	43	Grammar: past tense	1	
	44	Grammar: possessive pronouns	1	
	45	Punctuation: inverted commas	1	
	46	Punctuation: commas after fronted adverbials	1	
	47	Punctuation: inverted commas	1	
	48	Grammar: fronted adverbials	1	
	49	Grammar: Standard English	1	
Paper 2	1–20	Spelling	20	
		Total	**70**	

Marks & guidance

Marking and assessing the papers

Grammar, punctuation, vocabulary and spelling, where appropriate in the tests, have right/wrong answers. However, there are some open-ended questions that require the children's input. For these questions, example answers have been provided. They are not exhaustive and alternatives may be appropriate, so careful marking and a certain degree of interpretation will be needed.

Marking paper 1: questions

Question type	Accept	Do not accept
Tick boxes	Clear unambiguous marks.	Responses where more boxes have been ticked than required.
Circling or underlining	Clear unambiguous indication of the correct answer – including a box.	Responses where more than the required number of words have been circled or underlined. Responses where the correct answer is circled or underlined, together with surrounding words. Answers in which less than half of the required word is circled or underlined.
Drawing lines	Lines that do not touch the boxes, provided the intention is clear.	Multiple lines drawn to or from the same box (unless a requirement of the question).
Labelling parts of speech	Clear labels, whether they use the full vocabulary required by the question or an unambiguous abbreviation.	Ambiguity in labelling such as the use of 'CN' when asked to identify collective nouns and common nouns.
Punctuation	Punctuation that is clear, unambiguous and recognisable as the required punctuation mark.	Punctuation that is ambiguous, for example if it is unclear whether the mark is a comma or full stop.
Spelling	Where no specific mark scheme guidance is given, incorrect spellings of the correct response should be accepted.	Correct spelling is generally required for questions assessing contracted forms, plurals, verb tenses, prefixes and suffixes.

Marking paper 2: spelling

- If more than one attempt is made, it must be clear which version the child wishes to be marked.

- Spellings can be written in upper or lower case, or a mixture of the two.

- If a word has been written with the correct sequence of letters but they have been separated into clearly divided components, with or without a dash, the mark should not be awarded.

- If a word has been written with the correct sequence of letters but an apostrophe or hyphen has been inserted, the mark should not be awarded.

- Any acceptable British-English spelling can be marked as correct. For example, *organise* or *organize*.

Marks table

At the end of each test there is a table for you to insert the number of marks achieved for each question. This will enable you to see which areas your child needs to practise further.

National standard in Grammar, Punctuation & Spelling

The mark that the child gets in the test paper will be known as the 'raw score' (for example, '38' in 38/70). The raw score will be converted to a scaled score and children achieving a scaled score of 100 or more will achieve the national standard in that subject. These 'scaled scores' enable results to be reported consistently year-on-year.

The guidance in the table below shows the marks that children need to achieve to reach the national standard. This should be treated as a guide only as the number of marks may vary. You can also find up-to-date information about scaled scores on our website: www.scholastic.co.uk/nationaltests

Marks achieved	Standard
0–37	Has not met the national standard in Grammar, Punctuation & Spelling for Year 4
38–70	Has met the national standard in Grammar, Punctuation & Spelling for Year 4

Q	Answers	Marks
1	(on) (friday) (eva) went running.	1
2	The <u>teacher</u> gave out sparkly <u>stickers</u>.	1
3	The girls were playing in the long, green grass.	1
4	The boy stood on the stage (confidently).	1
5	I played on the swing, the slide and the climbing frame.	1

6   Marks: 1

	Past tense	Present tense
The enormous dog barked at the postwoman.	✓	
I walk to school.		✓
The baby slept in his cot.	✓	

Q	Answers	Marks
7	Any adjective that is appropriate to the sentence, for example: The girl wore a **beautiful / short / blue** dress. (Or lovely, nice, pretty, long, yellow, horrid, cool, frilly and so on.)	1
8	Rosie am / are / were / (was) running late for football practice but we started anyway.	1
9	It was a hot day <u>and</u> the children were playing in the garden.	1

10   Marks: 1

What a mess your room is! → Exclamation
Could you tidy your room? → Question
Tidy up this mess now. → Command
There are a lot of things on your bedroom floor. → Statement

11   Marks: 1

	New word
obey	disobey
appear	**disappear**
agree	**disagree**
like	**dislike**

Q	Answers	Marks
12	Adverb of time	1
13	I go to dance lessons on Saturdays**,** Sundays and Tuesdays.	1

■SCHOLASTIC National Curriculum SATs Tests

Q	Answers	Marks
14		1

Verb	Noun
teach	teacher
dance	**dancer**
run	**runner**

Q	Answers	Marks
15		1

I am → I'm
do not → don't
I will → I'll
you are → you're

Q	Answers	Marks
16	He ate <u>the last chocolate cupcake</u>. Accept if 'the' is not underlined but the rest of the phrase is.	1
17	The children splashed in the puddles (when) it rained.	1
18		1

	Possession	Contraction
I don't like swimming.		✓
The teacher found Adam's PE bag.	✓	
You're really good at swimming.		✓

Q	Answers	Marks
19	I am running in the playground.	1
20		1

✓   ☐ ✓   ☐
Line up please, said the teacher.

Q	Answers	Marks
21	I saw a shiny, blue bike (in) the shop window.	1
22		1

	Main clause	Subordinate clause
I saw a beautiful rainbow in the sky **when the sun shone**.		✓
When it rained, **the children splashed in the puddles**.	✓	
We had a picnic outside **because it was sunny**.		✓

Q	Answers	Marks
23		1

child	solve
children	solution
childlike	dissolve
childish	insoluble

Q	Answers	Marks
24	"What is the time please?" asked Farah.	I
25	The girl chose (a) / an pear from the fruit bowl.	I
26	The birds sing beautifully.	I
27	While at the park, I played on the swings.	I
28	I am going to tidy (my) room.	I
29	Any fronted adverbial that is appropriate to the sentence. For example: Under a large tree, Under the red umbrella.	I
30	The dog barks at the cat.	I
31	Tidy your room.	I
32	The frog **hopped** into the pond.	I
33	What time do lessons start? / Do lessons start at 9 o'clock? or similar. Must have a question mark.	I
34	The little boy ran to the finish line (as fast as he could).	I
35	Yesterday, I had toast for breakfast.	I
36	girls'	I
37	"How old are you?" asked the lady behind the desk.	I
38	An adverb	I
39	The nurse measured (Ava's) temperature.	I
40	I <u>went</u> to the cinema at the weekend.	I
41	hot chocolate with marshmallows → a noun phrase / an adverbial phrase / a prepositional phrase	I
42	(Before) dinner, she washed her hands.	I
43	You can borrow my sunglasses **but** be careful not to break them.	I
44	Callum was upset that <u>he</u> couldn't go to the party.	I
45	What a brilliant cartwheel the gymnast did	I
46	Andrew has been to rugby practice before.	I
47	is was	I
48	The last chocolate was (mine).	I
49	Ella <u>accidentally</u> broke her mother's favourite vase.	I
50	"What would you like to drink?" asked the waiter.	I
	Total	50

SCHOLASTIC National Curriculum SATs Tests

Test A, Paper 2:
Spelling test script and mark scheme

This spelling test can be found on pages 28–30.

Notes for conducting the spelling test

The task should take approximately **15 minutes** to complete, although you should allow children as much time as they need to complete it.

Read the instructions below to the children.

> *Listen carefully to the instructions I am going to give you.*
>
> *I am going to read you 20 sentences. Each sentence has a word missing. You should listen carefully to the missing word and fill this in, making sure you spell it correctly.*
>
> *I will read the word, then the word within a sentence, then repeat the word a third time.*
>
> *Do you have any questions?*
>
> Then read the spellings to the children as follows:
>
> **1.** Give the spelling number.
>
> **2.** Say 'The word is...'.
>
> **3.** Read the context sentence.
>
> **4.** Repeat 'The word is...'.
>
> Leave at least a 12-second gap between spellings.
>
> At the end, re-read all 20 questions. Then say *This is the end of the test please put down your pen or pencil.*

Each correct answer should be awarded **1 mark**. For more information on marking this task, please refer to page 77.

Spelling one: the word is **February**.

In **February**, it snowed heavily for days.

The word is **February**.

Spelling two: the word is **grate**.

Can you **grate** the cheese?

The word is **grate**.

Spelling three: the word is **measure**.

The builder needed to **measure** the room.

The word is **measure**.

Spelling four: the word is **decision**.

I had to make a **decision** about which after-school club to go to.

The word is **decision**.

Spelling five: the word is **information**.

The tour guide gave us lots of **information** about the museum.

The word is **information**.

Spelling six: the word is **happily**.

The girl danced **happily** across the room.

The word is **happily**.

Spelling seven: the word is **misleading**.

The sign was **misleading** because it pointed in the wrong direction.

The word is **misleading**.

Spelling eight: the word is **incorrect**.

The teacher said the answer was **incorrect**.

The word is **incorrect**.

Spelling nine: the word is **piece**.

My sister ate the last **piece** of fruit.

The word is **piece**.

Spelling ten: the word is **different**.

Although they are twins, Mia and Ava are quite **different**.

The word is **different**.

Spelling eleven: the word is **promise**.

I **promise** to do my homework.

The word is **promise**.

Spelling twelve: the word is **potatoes**.

I had **potatoes** for dinner.

The word is **potatoes**.

Spelling thirteen: the word is **interest**.

The boy read his magazine with **interest**.

The word is **interest**.

Spelling fourteen: the word is **imagine**.

Imagine flying to the moon in a rocket.

The word is **imagine**.

Spelling fifteen: the word is **build**.

We learned how to **build** a wall.

The word is **build**.

Spelling sixteen: the word is **library**.

I borrowed a book from the **library**.

The word is **library**.

Spelling seventeen: the word is **favourite**.

My **favourite** colour is blue.

The word is **favourite**.

Spelling eighteen: the word is **exercise**.

Exercise is good for your body and heart.

The word is **exercise**.

Spelling nineteen: the word is **accident**.

There was a car **accident** on the motorway.

The word is **accident**.

Spelling twenty: the word is **remember**.

I can't **remember** my password to log on to the computer.

The word is **remember**.

Test B, Paper 1: Questions mark scheme (pages 32–49)

Q	Answers	Marks
1	The little brown (hamster) had escaped from his (cage.)	1
2	An adjective	1
3		1

Would you like a drink? → Question

I had a drink. → Statement

What a refreshing drink that was! → Exclamation

Get me a drink. → Command

Q	Answers	Marks
4	(on) (wednesdays) (i) have drumming lessons.	1
5	The <u>new</u> computer was <u>large</u> and <u>gleaming</u>.	1
6		1

	Full stop	Question mark
When will the football match start		✓
When we walked to school, it was very cold	✓	
When can I eat my lunch		✓

Q	Answers	Marks
7	I didn't like my lunch and / (but) / or I enjoyed the pudding.	1
8	A noun	1
9	playing	1
10	I packed an umbrella, Wellington boots and a coat.	1
11	The boy am / are / were / (was) singing.	1
12		1

un → happy

im → possible

dis → like

in → correct

Q	Answers	Marks
13	I had sandwiches, an apple and a drink for lunch.	1
14	My sister took <u>the last piece of fruit</u>. Accept if 'the' isn't underlined but the rest of the phrase is.	1

| **15** | | |

Adjective	Adverb
slow	slowly
quick	**quickly**
careful	**carefully**
excited	**excitedly**

Marks: 1

16	The teacher found Annie's lunchbox in the hall.	1
17	While I **was reading** a book, my sister **was playing** with her toy car.	1
18	Any suitable adverb, for example loudly, often.	1

19

Marks: 1

20	even though	1
21	I woke up (before) my alarm clock.	1
22	**appear**: disappear, reappear, appearance **cycle**: bicycle, tricycle, cyclist, recycle Accept any other appropriate answers.	1
23	It hurt (when I fell over in the playground).	1
24	At playtime I had **an** orange.	1
25		1

✓   ☐ ✓   ☐

Are we nearly there yet? asked the little boy.

26	Khaled went home early. He took her / (his) / him bag with him.	1
27	As it was raining, we played games in the classroom.	1
28	That bird ate some seeds on the bird table.	1

Q	Answers	Marks
29	I cooked dinner for my friends.	1

| 30 | | | | | 1 |

Sentence	Statement	Question	Command
When can we sit down		✓	
Sit down			✓
It's great to sit down	✓		

Q	Answers	Marks
31	The baby **sleeps** in her cot.	1
32	Accept any statement such as: You should eat your sandwiches before your cake.	1
33	fronted adverbial or adverbial of time	1
34	I (have) white shoes.	1
35	"Can i play?" asked gemma.	1
36	"**W**hat time do you normally go to bed?" asked **A**jay. "**U**sually around 8.00pm," replied **I**saac.	1
37	The children were playing (outdoors).	1
38	What an amazing day we've had	1
39	George was crying at lunchtime.	1
40	He ran through the woods quick / (quickly).	1
41	I ate a boiled egg with a runny yolk for my breakfast. Accept if 'a' is not underlined but the rest of the phrase is.	1
42	I tidied my room **so** I could have my pocket money.	1
43	"That is (mine)," shouted the child.	1
44	After dinner, we read a story together.	1
45	was is	1
46	Since last year, Cora has wanted to be on the cricket team.	1
47	After swimming, we had a picnic.	1
48	"Make sure all the litter goes in the bin please," said the teacher.	1
49	✓ ↓ After school on Tuesdays I have judo and then football.	1
50	"It is extremely likely to rain this afternoon," said the weather presenter.	1
	Total	**50**

Test B, Paper 2:
Spelling test script and mark scheme

This spelling test can be found on pages 50–52.

Notes for conducting the spelling test

The task should take approximately **15 minutes** to complete, although you should allow children as much time as they need to complete it.

Read the instructions below to the children.

Listen carefully to the instructions I am going to give you.

I am going to read you 20 sentences. Each sentence has a word missing. You should listen carefully to the missing word and fill this in, making sure you spell it correctly.

I will read the word, then the word within a sentence, then repeat the word a third time.

Do you have any questions?

Then read the spellings to the children as follows:

1. Give the spelling number.

2. Say 'The word is...'.

3. Read the context sentence.

4. Repeat 'The word is...'.

Leave at least a 12-second gap between spellings.

At the end, re-read all 20 questions. Then say *This is the end of the test please put down your pen or pencil.*

Each correct answer should be awarded **1 mark**. For more information on marking this task, please refer to page 77.

Spelling one: the word is **perhaps**.

Perhaps it will be sunny at the weekend.

The word is **perhaps**.

Spelling two: the word is **mane**.

The lion's **mane** was long and fluffy.

The word is **mane**.

Spelling three: the word is **picture**.

I stuck the **picture** onto the fridge.

The word is **picture**.

Spelling four: the word is **television**.

I was watching **television**.

The word is **television**.

Spelling five: the word is **sensation**.

Walking on the grass with bare feet was a strange **sensation**.

The word is **sensation**.

Spelling six: the word is **finally**.

Finally, I finished my homework.

The word is **finally**.

Spelling seven: the word is **misbehave**.

The teacher warned us not to **misbehave** on the school trip.

The word is **misbehave**.

Spelling eight: the word is **impossible**.

The test was **impossible**.

The word is **impossible**.

Spelling nine: the word is **hear**.

Did you **hear** that noise?

The word is **hear**.

Spelling ten: the word is **various**.

The shelves were covered in lots of plants and shrubs of **various** shapes and sizes.

The word is **various**.

Spelling eleven: the word is **arrived**.

The post had **arrived** on time.

The word is **arrived**.

Spelling twelve: the word is **believe**.

I didn't **believe** the story.

The word is **believe**.

Spelling thirteen: the word is **early**.

I woke up very **early** this morning.

The word is **early**.

Spelling fourteen: the word is **enough**.

Is there **enough** paper for everyone?

The word is **enough**.

Spelling fifteen: the word is **disappear**.

Scissors don't just **disappear**.

The word is **disappear**.

Spelling sixteen: the word is **guards**.

We saw the **guards** outside Buckingham palace.

The word is **guards**.

Spelling seventeen: the word is **naughty**.

My cousin was very **naughty** at the supermarket.

The word is **naughty**.

Spelling eighteen: the word is **special**.

I was allowed to stay up late as it was a **special** occasion.

The word is **special**.

Spelling nineteen: the word is **material**.

We investigated which **material** would be best for an umbrella.

The word is **material**.

Spelling twenty: the word is **learn**.

I would like to **learn** Spanish.

The word is **learn**.

Test C, Paper 1: Questions mark scheme (pages 54–70)

Q	Answers	Marks
1	(Zara) ate a juicy (pear).	1
2	When is it lunch time**?** What a brilliant lunch**!** Lunch is at 1 o'clock today**.**	1
3	A noun	1
4	The wind blew my (favourite) kite into the (old) (oak) tree.	1
5	We was / (were) / am running around the playground at lunchtime.	1
6	<table><tr><th>Adjective</th><th>Adverb</th></tr><tr><td>**wobbly** **ancient** **shiny**</td><td>carefully **next** **gently**</td></tr></table>	1
7	(last) (thursday,) (i) went to the park.	1
8	happi**ly**	1
9	I packed a towel, my goggles and a swimming costume.	1
10	unkind, unpleasant, unhappy	1
11	Any suitable adverb of time, for example Often, Regularly, Sometimes.	1
12	<table><tr><th></th><th>New word</th></tr><tr><td>prepare</td><td>preparation</td></tr><tr><td>sense</td><td>**sensation**</td></tr><tr><td>admire</td><td>**admiration**</td></tr></table>	1
13	she is → she's he has → he's I have → I've we are → we're	1
14	I **was reading** my book while the teacher **was talking**.	1
15	The tired little girl fell asleep on the way home. Accept if 'the' is not underlined but the rest of the phrase is.	1

SCHOLASTIC National Curriculum SATs Tests

Q	Answers				Marks
16		**Possession**	**Contraction**		I

	Possession	Contraction
I don't like art classes.		✓
The teacher found Jake's homework in his bag.	✓	
Amira's ballet shoes were lost.	✓	
I'm going to play netball at lunchtime.		✓

Q	Answers	Marks
17	<u>I didn't go to school today</u> because I was unwell.	I
18	"I have forgotten my PE kit," said Ted.	I
19	The towels were ⟨on⟩ the bathroom shelf.	I
20	We had a / <u>an</u> unusual fruit at snack time and <u>a</u> / an delicious orange drink.	I
21	The children were going on a school trip to the zoo. To prepare for their trip, he / she / ⟨they⟩ / we had written down questions to ask the zookeeper.	I
22	In the sunshine**,** we sat and waited for our lunch.	I
23	The boys were dancing.	I
24	There was ⟨a⟩ book token for ⟨every⟩ child.	I
25	The frog **kissed** the pretty princess.	I
26	Go home.	I

27

Present tense	Past tense
We know	We knew
We draw	We drew
We run	We ran

Marks: I

28

Is it time to go to school?	Statement
It's time to go to school.	Exclamation
Go to school.	Question
What an amazing school this is!	Command

(Is it time to go to school? → Question; It's time to go to school. → Statement; Go to school. → Command; What an amazing school this is! → Exclamation)

Marks: I

Q	Answers	Marks
29	Last Sunday, my granny took me to the zoo.	I

Q	Answers	Marks
30	**a.**	1

	New word
turn	return
decorate	**redecorate**
appear	**reappear**

Q	Answers	Marks
	b. *re* means to do again or 'back'. For example, 'return' means to come back, 'redecorate' means to decorate again, and 'reappear' means to come back or appear again. (Accept any response that shows an understanding that *re* means again or back and changes the meaning of a word in this way.)	1
31	The Eiffel Tower is in France.	1
32	**W**hen the children arrived at the airport, they were excited**.** **T**hen they found out that their flight was delayed for two hours**.** **W**hen they finally arrived in **S**pain, they were very tired**.**	1
33	"What are we having for lunch**?**" Rachel asked.	1
34	A verb	1
35	The (optician) tested my (eyes.)	1
36	<u>Often</u>, I go swimming on Saturdays.	1
37	a lovely cup of tea → a noun phrase a prepositional phrase an adverbial phrase a noun phrase	1
38	<u>Because</u> it was so hot, we put sun cream on.	1
39	You can visit the dinosaur museum **but** you mustn't touch anything.	1
40	(We) had ice creams and (they) all had chocolate sauce on top.	1
41	What a wonderful party I went to	1
42	Aryan has been waiting the longest.	1
43	We **wrote** emails to our grandparents. We **drew** pictures when we **got** bored.	1
44	At the shop we all bought new hats. (Mine) is blue.	1
45	"I was second in the skipping race on Sports Day," said Sally happily.	1
46	After painting**,** wash the brushes with warm water.	1
47	**"**No running by the pool,**"** said the lifeguard.	1
48	After the countdown, the rocket launched into space.	1
49	The children was / (were) having a picnic at the park.	1
	Total	**50**

SCHOLASTIC National Curriculum SATs Tests

This spelling test can be found on pages 71–73.

Notes for conducting the spelling test

The task should take approximately **15 minutes** to complete, although you should allow children as much time as they need to complete it.

Read the instructions below to the children.

Listen carefully to the instructions I am going to give you.

I am going to read you 20 sentences. Each sentence has a word missing. You should listen carefully to the missing word and fill this in, making sure you spell it correctly.

I will read the word, then the word within a sentence, then repeat the word a third time.

Do you have any questions?

Then read the spellings to the children as follows:

1. Give the spelling number.

2. Say 'The word is...'.

3. Read the context sentence.

4. Repeat 'The word is...'.

Leave at least a 12-second gap between spellings.

At the end, re-read all 20 questions. Then say *This is the end of the test please put down your pen or pencil.*

Each correct answer should be awarded **1 mark**. For more information on marking this task, please refer to page 77.

Spelling one: the word is **purpose**.

My cousin damaged the kite on **purpose**.

The word is **purpose**.

Spelling two: the word is **break**.

I hoped the wobbly chair would not **break**.

The word is **break**.

Spelling three: the word is **creature**.

There was a tiny red and black **creature** crawling on the window sill.

The word is **creature**.

Spelling four: the word is **invasion**.

The **invasion** began in the middle of the night.

The word is **invasion**.

Spelling five: the word is **presentation**.

The **presentation** of your work is important.

The word is **presentation**.

Spelling six: the word is **carefully**.

I **carefully** put the ladybird back outside.

The word is **carefully**.

Spelling seven: the word is **misheard**.

I was lost because I had **misheard** the directions.

The word is **misheard**.

Spelling eight: the word is **disagreed**.

I **disagreed** with my brother's choice of television programme.

The word is **disagreed**.

Spelling nine: the word is **leaves**.

The autumn **leaves** were blowing around the playground.

The word is **leaves**.

Spelling ten: the word is **consider**.

I will **consider** my answer.

The word is **consider**.

Spelling eleven: the word is **breath**.

I held my **breath**.

The word is **breath**.

Spelling twelve: the word is **completed**.

I finally **completed** my homework.

The word is **completed**.

Spelling thirteen: the word is **continue**.

"Please **continue**," said the teacher.

The word is **continue**.

Spelling fourteen: the word is **famous**.

I want to be a **famous** singer.

The word is **famous**.

Spelling fifteen: the word is **forward**.

I was facing **forward** on the train.

The word is **forward**.

Spelling sixteen: the word is **heard**.

I **heard** a strange noise outside.

The word is **heard**.

Spelling seventeen: the word is **heart**.

Exercise raises your **heart** rate.

The word is **heart**.

Spelling eighteen: the word is **island**.

The boat arrived at the desert **island**.

The word is **island**.

Spelling nineteen: the word is **ordinary**.

It was just an **ordinary** day.

The word is **ordinary**.

Spelling twenty: the word is **women**.

The **women** were chatting loudly in the cafe.

The word is **women**.

QUICK TESTS FOR SATs SUCCESS

BOOST YOUR CHILD'S CONFIDENCE WITH 10-MINUTE SATs TESTS

- Bite-size mini SATs tests which take just 10 minutes to complete
- Covers key National Test topics
- Full answers and progress chart provided to track improvement
- Available for Years 1 to 6

Find out more at www.scholastic.co.uk